Hawk Sighting

by

Alfred Willowhawk

Original Art by Ziza

First Edition
First Printing, 2007

Original Artwork by Ziza © 2007
http://www.zizaart.com

Published by *Willowhawk Press*
Lawrence, KS
http://www.vajrasattvasavitur.com

ISBN: 978-0-6151-8338-1

This work is dedicated to the Goddess who inspires me every single day, my partner Lisa, as well as David, Denise, Dawn, Robert, Carl, Lily and Gary, who demonstrated their love for me by supporting, and encouraging me in this project.

Darkwing Series

Darkwing 1 © by a willowhawk 06-03-07

Darkwinged Spirit of the Light
Doomed existence Firewinged
Least remembered find the sight
Lady sprite of gold tinged dream
Drops like rain upon the stream

Light winged spirit of the night
Light winged spirit reaching beauty
Blue eyed Fire Burning bright
Leave remorse below the surface

Light winged Spirit of the Night
Sitting thinking broad winged beauty
Azure lining reaching stretching
Leave off sadness
Heartfelt striving
Otherworld being
Always seen and always hidden

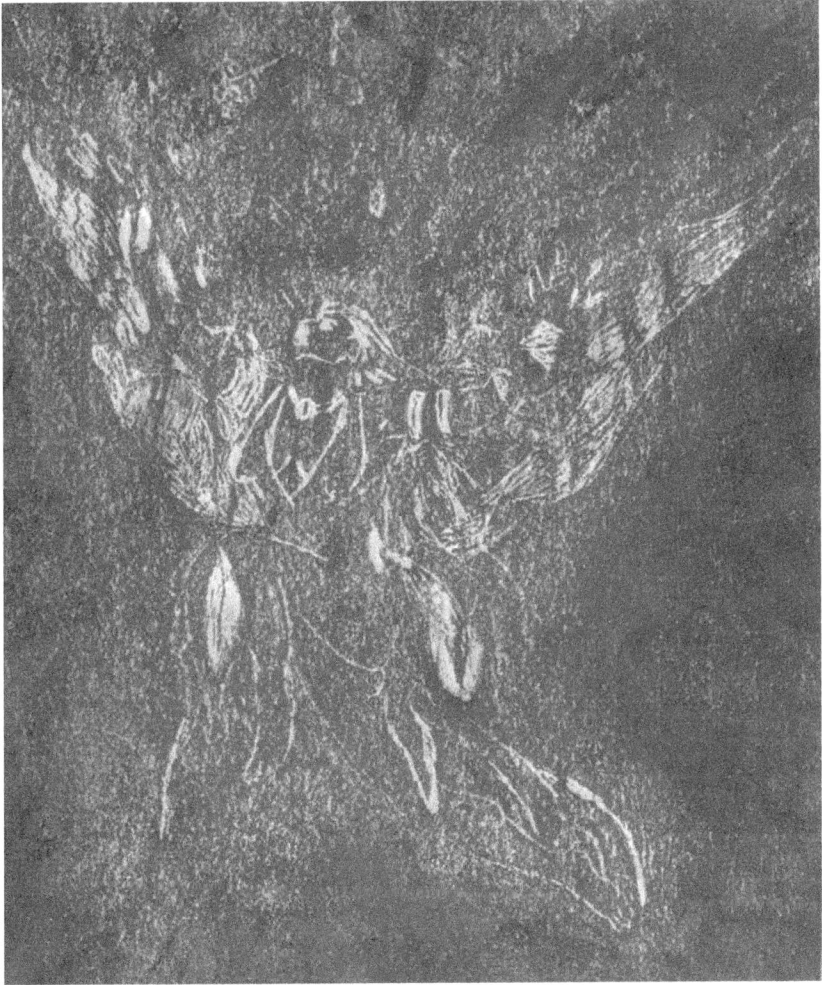

Darkwing 2 © by a willowhawk 06-03-07

Sitting still on Rock strewn shore
River raging from the storm
Sits there hidden in plain sight
Fey born princess dark and light
What's her thoughts as sun dew falls
Lovers found that break down walls
Flash of darkness as she dives
Blue eyes flashing shows she lives
Breasts turned upward catch the sun
Smiling softly as she lunged
Can you see her in Sun's bright dew?
Or can you follow paths that bring you
through.

Darkwing 3 © by a willowhawk 06-03-07

Ponderous Silence waits for something
Straining meekly toward the waiting
Intensely expectant for Mornings breaking

Sun light hid behind the cloude
Nature nourishes, life and comb
Where have you gone
And why are you waiting?

Untitled Series

Untitled © by a willowhawk 05-03-07

Silence broken like rain on concrete
Darkness broken when moon beams flow
Raging silence that stills the child
Wounds to deep to heal and smile
Mother's tears and fathers bellow

Crumbling walls that never stood
Hearing mourns the waiting sunlight
Waiting still beside the stream
Catch the flash of expectant beauty

To the Beautiful Manifestation of the Goddess

New Beginnings © by a willowhawk 10-12-07

Feelings loosened, trust accepted
Expectant friendship Goddess driven

Wind is freshened
Sun breaks through
Leaves of Gold and Blue revealed
Reach the wheel and watch it turn
Man is fleeting She remains

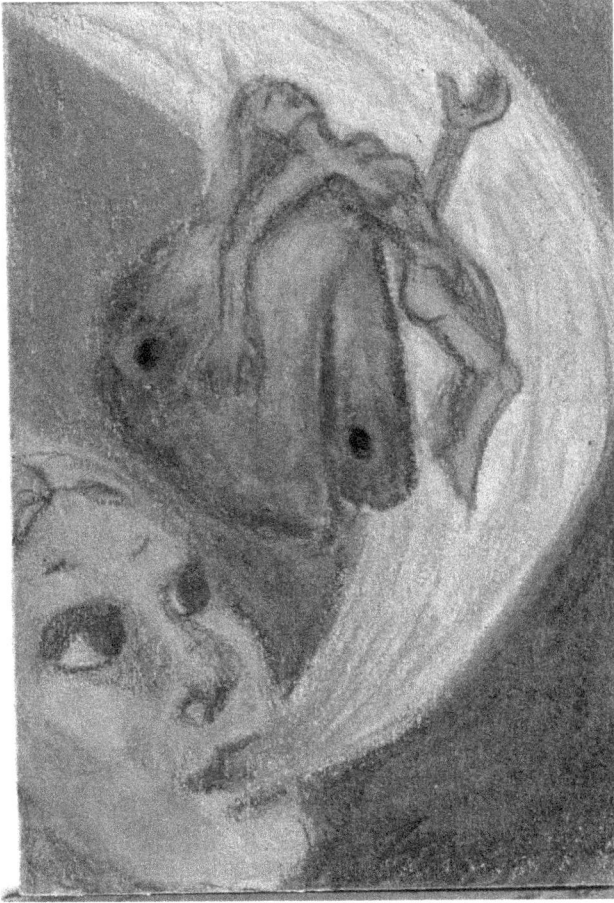

Trust © by a willowhawk 10-12-07

Revealed and Hidden
Emotion Driven
Where's the Balance
Mind and Soul

We are learning
While others don't
Leave off dying
Live for trying
Made of dreams, life and being

Merging all to mother greet
While she gives and never takes
Always there to show the way
Never forcing always churning

Can we wait on love's embrace?

The Fey Series

Fey 1 © by a willowhawk 10-05-07

Smiling Eyes of cleares morning
Voice that tinkles water flowing
Earth based scents of the Goddess
Come to me the earswhile being

Pearly whites that light the night
Streaks of wheat that ripple ripple
Laughter shines up to the heavens
Moonlit Goddess still as night

Fey 2 © by a willowhawk 10-08-07

Broken Strands of spider's center
Flash of Violet desiring Truth
Pull the power ever downward
Bring forth Love that never dies

Broken strips of Life and Love
Healing centers scars unfolding
Laughing, loosening soon to yield
Strands to center spider whole

Fey Princess © by a willowhawk 11-11-06

Fey of the Glen
Hills of amber
Bringer of the Sun
Shaft winged virtue
Poignant disappointment
Re-assemble to staff
Release the Stag of Truth
Accept the Lesson to bring true healing
Reassemble the council under the hill
Manifest the Glory
Restore the Land
Mother of Many
Master of none
Leave of desire
Control and thought
Fey of the Glen
Strengthen the Dragon
Spider of Pathways
Otherworld gateway
Live on both the bright and low
Bring forth Light and Love
Goddess all
Reassemble the council under the hill
Manifest the Glory

Restore the Land
Mother of Many
Master of none
Leave off desire
Control and thought
Fey of the Glen
Subjugate your control
Bring forth desire through love and truth
Bearer of death
protector of power
Control self to be self
Caller of the way
Reassemble the council under the hill
Manifest the Glory
Restore the Land
Mother of Many
Master of none
Leave off desire
Control and thought
Fey of Dragon, Owl and Wolf
Listen to the calling
Choose the path of truth
Make for the castle under the hill
Amber Glory
Lapis Truth

Poems from Oklahoma City

These poems were inspired by the glass work of Dale Chihuly on display in the Oklahoma City Museum of Art. *Winged Beauty* was inspired by the Eleanor Blake Kirkpatrick Memorial Tower, *Mother Love* by Autumn Gold Persian Wall and Tiger Lily installation, and *Soul Retrieval* by Neodymium Reeds.

Winged Beauty – 7 07 07 © by a willowhawk

Towering Beauty
Flowering Light
Left on Center
Twirling swans
Reach the Sky
Draw down the moon
Ageless wonder
Swan Song's delight

Reaching Upward toward the Sun
Turning, Singing, arcing tiger
Willowed Branchings
Leap for Joy
Slithering outward
Grasping rainbows
forever trapped in time

Mother Love – 7 07 07 © by a willowhawk

Polyps Reaching
Tentacles Upward
Thrusting, straining
Faceless columns
Bulbous Fingers
Forrest of Spirals
Balanced Downward
Anchor reality
a cloud form parody

Iridescent wombs
Floating Free
embrace the Airways
Crystalline dancers
Loving Life
the Mother cautions
REJOICE in Beauteous Freedom
Web of Life complete

Soul Retrieval – 7 07 07 © a willowhawk

SHATTERED Trunks of the Mother
Lost arms forever gone
rootless now crying from ecstacy
laying gasping, choking, sapless, silent
embracing darkness soon to come

Spirit Crys!!!
Thrusts out from the body
Quiet Thunder EXPLODES toward the cosmos
Life force reaching- Mother -   where and why??

Purple fingers sparks of life
Straining reaching straight and light
Mother hears and cries – You too??
Encircling Love – come home come home

Winged Watcher © by a willowhawk 06-03-07

Purple White Entwining Spirit
Crystal Wings that flash with Power
Diving, acting, Listening roar
Quiet Thunder
Water Flashing
Reaching always to the Light

Fire Series

Fire 1 © a willowhawk 10-26-07

Fire Thread climbing
Reach for the Gloom
Fingers dancing
Consuming Desire
Burn forever
Fueless wonder
Sustaining Life Force
Beacon of Remembrance

Fire 2 © a willowhawk

Doorway Beacon
Beckoning Brightly
Hidden Pathways
Dragon Waiting
Golden wings
That beat from glory
Calling forth the erstwhile mourning.

Leave off dying
Sleep for now
Wait the dawn
Of new-tide dawning

Fire 3 10-26-07 © a willowhawk

Embered Promise
Lover's embrace
Death brings light
And light harkens death
Fallen fairies
Rebirth ensured
FLASH! A flamelight
Consuming passion

Fire 4 10-26-07 © a willowhawk

Earthbound Sprite
That shields the water
Burning deeply
Forgetting nothing
Forgiving all
Dew Bright threads
Lit from below
Fires raging
Encompassing love

The Call

The Call 10-26-07 © a willowhawk

Ringing Bells that promise freedom
People running
Full of hope

Deceitful Bells that entomb freedom
Lock and chain that
Blocks the day

Consuming passion to be free
Break the chains that darken eyes

Wishful thinking of slothful beings
Hear the bells that make the prison

People suffer
Rain ensues
Goddess beckons through freedoms toll

Goddess blest
Destroyer come
Shouting silence of prisons lost

Beings bereft of Goddess Glory
Remember TRUTH and Freedom's silence

Sacred Knots

KNOWLEDGE WISDOM AUTHORITATIVE BALANCE

Sacred Knots – 10-26-07 © a willowhawk

Life threads entwined
Beings pall
Creating knots that hide in Love

Hateful Liars
Self serving prophets
Twisting Life threads
Creating voids
Mock the sacred Knots of HER

Sacred knots that bring us peace
Trust and love that survive the Fall
Cycles waiting for the goddess
Glowing life threads evermore

For My Partner

For my partner – 10-26-07 © a willowhawk

Sleeping Fairy
Blest of Fire
Smiles freely
Love ensured

Stretch to waken
From your slumber
Wheat fields shimmering
With mornings blessing

Turn your eyes of purest water
Giving life to highest Fire

Wings encircling
Feeding growing
Love's sweet savor
Exploding Life light

Wheel that turns
And opens doorways
Springs sweet promise
Yet a way

Golden Fire off to sleeping
Dreams of spring times promised coming

Encircling Wings that hearken futures
Sleeping fire that waits for dawn
Remembers wheat and blue of water
Comes back safely when morn ensues.

Stone Stair Series

Little Feet © a willowhawk 11/13/07

Little feet Climbing
on Ancient pathways
forgotten realms that
lay there silent
on a world that doesn't see
Little feet pounding on silent tears

Steps that cry with forgotten glory
Left to ruin, spirits linger
Hills of mourning, hidden truths
while Little feet climb on broken dreams

Stone Work © a willowhawk 11/13/07

Stones of hour forgotten age
Power broken memory's sage
Lost inthoughts of ancient glory
not remembered life and story

Ancient Souls that have forgotten
New Life comes that was begotten
heaped upon the ancient wall
walked the paths that no on saw
Ancient Brother that breathes no more

The Sidhe © a willowhawk 11/13/07

Upward Surgng
hearing purging
Earstwhile sidhe
that stands unseen

Souls remembered pasts unfold
for the times of hills untold

Will you go on ancient mornings
Till the time of endless soaring?

Smallest spirit seeks the time
of endless summerland yet began

Will the day bring memory's gift
or still in wonder bringer of death

Autumn Series

Reaching © a willowhawk 11/13/07

naked branches ever weeping
Tossed by She who brings the sleep

Holly King awake at last
while the branches weep for pasts

Sleep eternal yet denied
To each spirit last unfolding
Winged and waiting goddess past
For awakening to the rast.

Weeping © a willowhawk 11/13/07

Golden tears that promise stillness
Blooded flesh that turns and shines
Sighing for the past entwined
with new beginnings to be refined

Naked arms that beckon upward
Call for summers yet unborn
Cycles, circles, roads refined
with footsteps left and paths defined

To The Maiden Huntress

The Huntress © a willowhawk 11/13/07

Drums that call across the veil
Awaken She that waits beyond
Feed the forest Love the dark
New come Maiden promised Love

Running free Protectress hunter
Watch for growth and halt the hurt
Leave off fighting watch for morning
Huntress goddess lover friend.

www.ingramcontent.com/pod-product-compliance
Lightning Source LLC
Chambersburg PA
CBHW030112070426

42448CB00036B/823